ALPHABET ANIMALS: ALPHABET BOOKS FOR TODDLERS

Speedy Publishing LLC
40 E. Main St. #1156
Newark, DE 19711
www.speedypublishing.com

A a

alligator

Bb

bear

C c

cat

Dd

donkey

E e

elephant

Ff

flamingo

Gg

giraffe

Hh

hippopotamus

Ii

iguana

J j

jaguar

Kk

kangaroo

Ll

lion

Mm

macaw

Nn

newt

Oo

ostrich

Pp

pig

Q q

quail

Rr

rhinoceros

S s

sheep

Tt

tiger

U u

urial

V v

vole

W w

wolf

X x

x-ray tetra

Y y

yak

Zz

zebra

What letter do the animals below starts with?

What letter do the animals below starts with?

What letter does the animal below starts with?